Butterflies

Aaron Frisch

CREATIVE EDUCATION

seedlings

Published by Creative Education
P.O. Box 227, Mankato, Minnesota 56002
Creative Education is an imprint of
The Creative Company
www.thecreativecompany.us

Design and production by Ellen Huber
Art direction by Rita Marshall
Printed in the United States of America

Photographs by Alamy (Roger Eritja), Dreamstime
(Melinda Fawver, Vladischern), Getty Images (Charles
Groux, Patricio Robles Gil/Sierra Madre, Oxford Scientific,
Steve Vincent), iStockphoto (arlindo71, Jiří Hodeček), Photo
Researchers (Stuart Wilson/Science Source), Shutterstock
(Olga Bogatyrenko, Barnaby Chambers, Butterfly Hunter, jps,
D. Kucharski K. Kucharska, Sari ONeal, Leena Robinson,
StevenRussellSmithPhotos), Veer (Vladimir Blinov, James
Laurie, Wong Sze Fei, Mihail Zhukov)

Library of Congress Cataloging-in-Publication Data
Frisch, Aaron.
Butterflies / Aaron Frisch.
p. cm. — (Seedlings)
Includes bibliographical references and index.
Summary: A kindergarten-level introduction to butterflies,
covering their growth process, behaviors, the warm areas they
call home, and such defining physical features as their wings.
ISBN 978-1-60818-457-6
1. Butterflies—Juvenile literature. I. Title.

QL544.2.F75 2014
595.78'9—dc23   2013029064

CCSS: RI.K.1, 2, 3, 4, 5, 6, 7;
RI.1.1, 2, 3, 4, 5, 6, 7; RF.K.1, 3; RF.1.1

First Edition
9 8 7 6 5 4 3 2 1

TABLE OF CONTENTS

Hello, butterflies!

Butterflies are flying bugs.
They live on trees.
They live in grassy places.
Butterflies like to be warm.

7

Butterflies have six legs and four wings. They have antennae on their heads.

Butterfly wings are soft. Many butterfly wings are pretty colors.

Butterflies eat nectar from flowers.

The nectar tastes sweet.

Baby butterflies are called

caterpillars.

They come
out of eggs.
Then they
become
butterflies.

Butterflies
fly from
flower
to flower.

They look
for food.
Then they
find a mate.

Goodbye, butterflies!

Picture a Butterfly

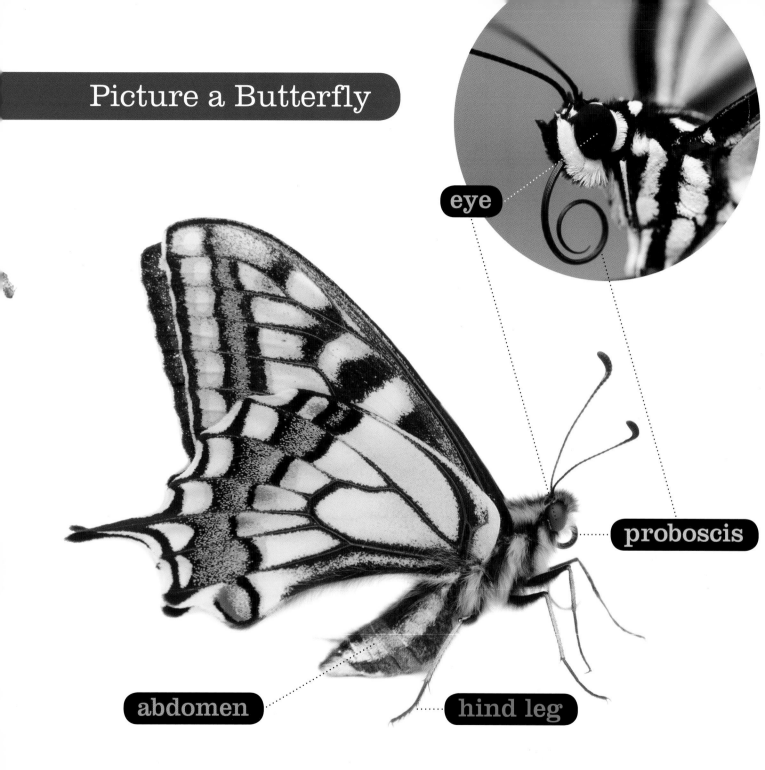

eye

proboscis

abdomen

hind leg

antennae

forewing

hind wing

scales

Words to Know

antennae: body parts that help a bug feel or smell things

caterpillars: the name for baby butterflies when they look like worms

mate: another animal to have babies with

nectar: a sweet liquid that flowers make

Read More

Marsh, Laura. *Caterpillar to Butterfly*.
Washington, D.C.: National Geographic, 2012.

Rustad, Martha E. H. *Butterflies*.
Minneapolis: Bellwether Media, 2008.

Websites

Butterfly Activities and Crafts
http://www.first-school.ws/theme/animals/
insects/butterfly.htm
Print out pictures of butterflies to color.

DLTK's Crafts for Kids: Butterflies and Caterpillars
http://www.dltk-kids.com/crafts/insects/butterflies.htm
Choose a craft to make a butterfly or caterpillar.

Index